Acrobats of Sound

Colin Pink

POETRY SALZBURG
at the University of Salzburg

SALZBURG

2016

First published in 2016 by Poetry Salzburg at the University of Salzburg

Editor: Wolfgang Görtschacher

ISBN: 978-3-901993-56-5

University of Salzburg
Department of English and American Studies
Unipark Nonntal
Erzabt-Klotz-Str. 1
5020 Salzburg
AUSTRIA

http://www.poetrysalzburg.com
editor@poetrysalzburg.com

Printed and bound in Germany by Offset Friedrich, Ubstadt-Weiher
(http://www.druckerei-friedrich.de/).

Contents

Acknowledgements

Some of the poems appeared in the following publications: "Whetstone" (*Poetry News*, Spring 2014), "Panther in the City" (*Ver Poetry Prize Anthology*, 2009), "Games the Dead Play" (*Ver Poetry Prize Anthology*, 2014), "Winter Trees Light" (*Equinox*, 2008), "The Pencil Fears the Eraser" (*THE SHOp*, 2011), "Five Painters" (*THE SHOp*, 2014), "Another Day, Another Pawn Ticket" and "Victorian Woman in a Green Dress" (*Poetry Salzburg Review* 25, Spring 2014), "Elegy for Dreamland" and "Water Clock" (*Lunar Poetry*, 2016), "Dragonflies" (*Urthona* 29, 2011), "The Double" (*Coffee House* 22, 2011 and *Ink, Sweat & Tears*, 2015), "Adelstrop or Elsewhere" (Poetry Society Website, 2014), "For Magritte, on a Rainy Day" (*Pen Pusher* 11, 2008), "Hammersmith Flyover" and "St Catherine Tekakwitha" (*South Bank Poetry* 24, 2016).

Many thanks to the editors of the above for their faith in my work. Thanks to Wolfgang for publishing the book.

Thank you to Jenny and everyone else (you know who you are) who have supported me in my writing.

Many thanks to Massimo Danielis for permission to use one of his wonderful etchings for the cover.

Many thanks to Caroline Kerslake for her expert photography.

ACROBATS OF SOUND

for Jenny

Panther in the City

There's a panther in the city: he paces the streets
and remembers all the faces that he meets, both
the sleek and the meek. He watches the sinew
and bone that you carry home with a hungry gaze
that shows he knows the hurt beneath the beauty.
A panther prowls the streets ready to strip the lies
from your soul; with razor-red claws in huge paws
he'll tear away the tattered shelter of your story.

He doesn't care if you're in a hurry or just killing time
as he sniffs out the stains that pain leaves behind.
He stalks every twist and turn of street and alley:
don't run or turn your back, for you're sure to feel the
heat of his breath on your neck. No fighting no fleeing,
welcome the panther within, turn your pelt into an offering.

Whetstone

I broke the whetstone,
　　knocked it off the shelf,
　　　　reaching for a book.

It fell to the floor,
　　broke in pieces with a
　　　　sharp clack and snap.

I fitted them together; they
　　balanced like drunks,
　　　　one on another.

Their razor sharp edges
　　made invisible joints
　　　　but at the merest touch

they fall apart again
　　exposing the wounds
　　　　of their separation.

My father was a barber,
　　it was his whetstone,
　　　　the surface worn concave,

honed by his hand,
　　year on year spent
　　　　sharpening the blade.

Watching him sharpening
　　the cut-throat razor
　　　　was a childhood fascination

as he spat on the stone
　　and ran the razor's edge
　　　　over it again and again

until it bore the shape
of his life; and still it
sharpens my memory.

Games the Dead Play

The dead hide behind tombstones
shy about the pallor of their bones.

They want to jump out and say hello
but are scared of swallowing your sorrow.

On birthdays they blow out other people's candles
and watch darkness descend from all angles.

They like to slide into your mind uninvited
and relish the way your mood gets blighted.

The dead like to be elusive and test
who among us remembers them best.

They look forward to the occasional visit
even from people whose purpose is illicit.

On their death day a party is started
but strictly only the dead are invited.

Shaman

He travels to other lands beyond the sky:
    walking to infinity
        discoursing with bears
sipping libations of ecstasy
    dancing on the rim of pain.

When he returns he brings back to the tribe:
    tales to weave
        gifts of healing
knowledge to knit
    news to share
greetings from the hare.

The shaman must rest   after his journey.
    Do not disturb him
        yet awhile;
    he has the moon to put back
        on its shelf to dry
and the stars to tidy away
    that have stuck to his cloak
        in the thicket of night.

He has the ancestors to see home again
        after too much feasting.
    Sometimes you see him   walking alone
but then it seems   there is more than one
    and now you see   a dance has begun.

Soon he'll travel again,
        gathering myths,
    like ripe fruit,
        peeled and ready to eat.

Winter   Trees   Light

The trunks of the trees,
moss grown, glow green in the
low winter light, bright without
heat.

The rings within the trunks
replay, like grooves in a record,
the mystery of good and bad
years.

Bare boughs outline this
cold blue sky, as though
grasping for something
forgotten.

The heat of the sun.
The mythic memory of sap.

Freeze Frame

At the top of the hill the wind claws my face; chill
thoughts rustle through me, dry as autumn leaves.

Every year winter returns, its freeze-dried breath
a vampire feeding, inducing anaemia of dreams.

Desire for hibernation casts long shadows, seduces
the mind with the urge to sup the dregs of sleep.

Someone pressed Pause and now everything seems
suspended, naked as a black bough against the sky.

Yet, hopes ascend, like a murmuration of starlings,
twisting and wringing fresh shadows from the sky.

Today I feel like an empty glove. Every path seems
a muddy palimpsest of aimless coming and going.

Time lies heavy as one of Dali's flaccid clocks
and weary feet lack traction to pull myself along.

Aspirations twirl downward, like sycamore seeds,
describing the beauty of their own slow descent.

A sparrow flies from the storm into the hall: in one door,
out the other, wears a blink of warmth between winters.

Field Path

For Caroline

The field path leads into the woods.
Blackthorn and briar, nature's barbed-wire,
scrawls across the muddy path;
curlicues of discomfort arrest us,
make us move slowly, as if underwater.
Light, filtered through leaves, clings
to the underside of boughs.
Rodents fidget the leaf-litter,
their startled movements summon
elemental alarm common to man and beast.
Deep inside the wood, where shadows
twitch in fitful dreams, the path
decays by degrees, becomes
no longer a route but reaches
a silent dead-end. A clearing
gathers around us, a dimple
of light, as we re-collect ourselves,
before turning back, retracing
steps that now seem so different,
no longer recognisably ours at all.

Metamorphosis

The trees that looked so sturdy yesterday today are uprooted.
The wind tugged the life from them. Now they are splayed
across the leaf-litter bed like the forensic outline of a victim.

But no one anywhere is investigating. Their strength was
an illusion, the heart of oak a dated dream, felled in one night
they revealed that reality is nothing like its surface gleam.

How many weathers have they worn? How many creatures
housed and fed? Now they are prone in death, home to beetles
and fungi. Yet still I glimpse some slow metamorphosis.

In the storm of days I listen for it, resisting all the evidence, losing
dreams of permanence, as all I thought of consequence falls away
and I stand clasping to me an unbuttoned coat of certainties.

The Pencil Fears the Eraser

The blind man's memory is touching.
A bone dreams of finding a buried dog.
The film stars' smiles go out at night.
A lighthouse dreams it's lost in fog.

A jug pours emptiness out of itself.
The ringing silence of the blue bells.
The true secretly loves the false.
A demon vacations to warmer hells.

A lost postcard misses the sea.
The ledge is scared to look down.
The weather never complains.
A fake smile betrays the frown.

A fish never sees the sea even on holiday.
The umbrella tingles at the touch of raindrops.
A letterbox swallows every word.
The stage is wary of anxious theatre props.

A clock is never impatient no matter how late.
A stone never hides its feelings.
The pencil fears the eraser is always behind it.
The paper slowly unfolds its meanings.

Pandora's Box

You would not know,
      to look at it,
what it is.
      A plain, unadorned,
      rather worn, wooden box.
No warning signs
attached to it.
      No Health & Safety
      stickers seal it.
No seal at all
protects it.
      It invites opening
      with mute resignation.
Go on, don't resist,
         open it;
      you know you want to.
Let's find out what's inside it;
you can't stand idle beside it.
      How does it feel
      when you touch it?
Is it cold or warm
      with some thing
         broiling within?
      What's that tapping I hear?
      O, just your impatient foot.
Go on, no one's looking,
      do it now!
         You know you'll feel
so much easier
      when everything is
         out in the open.

Sailing with Anubis

In the British Museum

I expected the sarcophagus to be empty
but instead a face looked back at me,
swaddled in bandages, brittle and white,
eyes and mouth stopped, locked in a night
full of ancient dreams, drifting in eddies
over the slippery contour of memories.

Such bodiless imagining, travelling light,
slipping down the Nile and out of sight;
what I saw wasn't a mummy but instead
a carved and bandaged marble head;
an uncanny echo of my expectation,
a finely carved mimetic deception.

The Egyptian galleries become a canopic jar
brimming with vital traces of who we are.
A silent relic serves as a dead letter box,
renders strange the present and unlocks
the imagination freed from chronology
to parse anxiety into fresh mythology.

Anubis needs to know how many tears
I spilled from others' eyes over the years.
And then he wants to weigh my heart
to judge how well I've played my part.
Only then can I pass through the veil
to the world of death and there set sail

to accompany the sun across the sky
on that final journey made after we die.
Safely embarked on the funerary boat
I open *The Book of the Dead*, as we float
across the sky, and chant my name
while the flames of dawn arise again.

The Treasure of the Sierra Madre

returns to the dry earth from which it came,
        dust to dust, ashes to ashes
blown on the wind, grain by precious grain.

The seeds of madness germinate in the sun,
        there's a season for everything,
while we labour to finish what was begun.

Who knows what is truly golden? A helping hand
        soothing the fevered eyes of need
like the tang of cooling water in a blistered land?

All that's left, at the end, is the insane laughter that just
        keeps on ringing in my memory
long after the actors themselves have turned to dust.

Gold Jug

From the Oxus Treasure, in the British Museum

Gold jug with your pouting lip,
>will you deign to give
>>me a precious kiss?

A lion's-head handle
>bites your rim; you
>>remain unflappable,

solid in the knowledge
>of your own worth.
>>No doubt you

belonged to someone
>important who wanted
>>everyone to know it.

Flutes, unfurling
>around your body,
>>accentuate the rise and

curve of your belly,
>full of light that's
>>throwing back

a honey slicked
>distillation of
>>day's pale rays.

But I detect an earthenware
>heart beating beneath
>>your polished surface.

Perhaps, after all,
>you were just
>>an ordinary jug

until one day Midas
      happened by and
            poured himself a drink.

Icarus & Us

Landscape with the Fall of Icarus by Pieter Bruegel

For Massimo

No one notices
        one tiny figure
                fall from the sky.

The ploughman's focus
        is on his furrow, he likes
                to get things straight.

The shepherd is a dreamer
        lost among his sheep,
                back turned to distress.

The ship sails away,
        brings no rescue
                to the struggling figure.

We all suspect our wings
        are too flimsy
                for extended flight,

attached merely with
        inadequate wax, and
                the sun rises every day

to whittle our bindings away.
        So Bruegel has painted
                the fate of Icarus and us:

to have our tragic demise
        ignored by the busy world,
                wiped out without significance:

the sun still shining,
      the birds still singing,
            the people out working;

nothing stops,
      time does not
            hesitate in its stride.

No one notices
      one tiny figure
            fall from the sky.

Another Day, Another Pawn Ticket

How the words bubble up, a logorrhoea,
like the frantic song of the skylarks,
out of control, spilling from the mouth,
tumbling together, heedless of art.

Such ecstatic music the Maenad's chanted
words to tear us limb from limb. We yield
but always stumble from the wreckage
then hitch a lift to another battlefield.

Miles Davis blows a smoky melody,
his trumpet becomes as soft and pliant
as a lover's lips wed to his for this brief
abandonment of original silence.

Some words are strong, some are weak,
yet bruises blossom beneath their touch.
Mapless, without direction, I ask myself
how we could have forgotten so much.

Pick-up moments, scattered pennies,
I want to place in the jar of memory
saved for some future time, a down-
payment on a long sought harmony.

Tear off a page from the calendar;
each leaf becomes, it would seem,
a pawn ticket to another moment
I'll never have the wealth to redeem.

Lamentation

Nini's Painting by Cy Twombly, 1971

not waves but
a forest
of feelings

calligraphy
of grief
spilling over

again a mist
of marks
with no meaning

not water
but drowning
here depicted

yet air
after all
can be found

hidden between
the marks
and behind

the feeling of panic
the frantic
rhythm of loss.

White Swan

When I left the pub all was right with the world;
the beer had been light and fruity, wrapped in the arms
of a refreshing bitterness, and I'd had just enough
to wash away anxieties without inviting fresh ones in.

The river brimmed and sparkled like good
conversation but something pungent grabbed
my attention. Fluid as the water in which it lies
the carcass of what had been a swan laps the bank.

This dishevelled shroud of feathers startles me
from my reverie; an emblem of poise and calm
now a shrill reminder that serenity is temporary.

Reduced to a scumble of tattered feathers this flightless
fletcher's arrows of mutability reek of liquefaction and
enter the realm of waste disposal; a kingdom for us all.

Victorian Woman in a Green Dress

Sogni by Vittorio Matteo Corcos, 1896

You look out defiantly as if to say, What
do you have for me? Impress me, go on.
You are waiting but your thoughts are elsewhere;

they drift free, like the loose strands of hair,
thought tendrils, that curl about your head.
What are you looking for, here on the bench?

Your eyes are not saying, nor your lips, as your
chin rests on the soft plinth of your hand, fingers
gloved in a second skin of supple leather.

Beside you the pile of books, in soft yellow covers,
suggests a taste for the decadent, the frisson of
forbidden literature and heat between the sheets.

This rendezvous was arranged long ago
and now we have forgotten why we came.
I am late and everything has time's patina upon it.

The leaves are etched with so many mottled
memories. And now I see the sorrow in your eyes.
Are you alive or an illusion of someone from long ago?

The leaves fall and petals wilt; the warmth of the day
retreats, chill night returns. Let's unwrap time, peel
back each brittle layer, until we might meet.

Composed on a Traffic Island

Standing on a traffic island, becalmed in mid-stream,
I'm surrounded by the pulsing waves of the Strand.
The siren's cacophony did not lure me onto this seam
but all the same, here I am, drowning on dry land.

Taxis swoop on pedestrians, like birds of prey;
their black plumage signals the price in this town
is higher than you think. At side-streets each day
traffic snarls at my heels, eager to run me down.

The CCTV's grainy evidence records the pace
I run my errands and hurry from place to place;
what's done and left undone both without grace.

Now I stand, shipwrecked on this reef, can I seek
the calm that lies beneath, hear the soul speak,
and find myself buried within the working week?

Sisyphus

Sisyphus grows to know his stone so well,
his face pressed against it like a lover,
as he pushes, pushes, upwards, always,

every sinew and bone screaming alone
in the baking heat and the driving sleet,
straining like one in labour for eternity.

The rock revolves before him each
and every day, like a blank clock it tells
no time but counts each moment.

He has memorised every pock and groove,
ridge and vein, on the face of his stone,
imprinted on his palms, kissing his cheek.

Each and every curve and crevice is carved
with a painful destiny in his memory, even
when he closes his eyes still he dreams it.

He knows it so well, its pulse is his pulse,
he grows a second skin of calluses the
better to kiss it on its way, day by day.

Till at the top, clothed in the sweat
of his journey, he can pause at last
on the summit and admire the view.

But the rock rolls down again, as it always
will. Camus tells us we must imagine
Sisyphus happy! The struggle upward,

toward the height, is enough to fill a man's
heart. But can we believe him, as we press
our face to the stone, each with our own?

The Haunted Letterbox

At the end of the long dark hallway
there is a letterbox;

its flap opens and shuts in the draught; beyond
the landing light

shines through – etching a slit in the door –
a grin of light

that mouths the words nobody utters –
I want to run

from its uncanny animation – accusing
clack of light –

which makes me ultra-aware of my
childhood wraith

caught in the spotlight's glare
barefoot and alone

shivering in striped pyjamas – afraid
of both light and dark.

Elegy for Dreamland

When I was a kid every summer
we'd go to Margate and visit
the amusement park called Dreamland.

They had this man, he guessed your weight,
and he always got it right. He felt you
all over, thoroughly, impersonally,
like a piece of meat, quickly, efficiently.

He felt your bones through your skin.
When he felt my bones I knew,
for the first time, I really existed.

American Civil War Bubblegum Cards

I learned all about the American Civil War
from the bubblegum cards. The gum
looked like thin strips of Elastoplast,
and after that first spearmint rush
turned to rubber in your mouth;
I never learned to blow the bubbles.

My brother and I collected the cards.
In the end, after snagging that elusive
missing card, we got the complete war.
This was in the late sixties; daily on the
evening news the Vietnam War was
played out, like a vivid tea-time movie.

We ate beans-on-toast or fish-fingers
while machine guns rattled and chopper
blades thrashed a stormy sea of foliage.
Marines ducked, crouched and ran through
long grass. Napalm illuminated the screen
like every firework display you'd ever seen.

Children came running, naked, down a thin
road, their thin arms outspread, their thin skin
burned off. They were being saved for freedom.
The American Civil War cards were just as
bloody but you could hold them in the palm
of your hand. Men in blue and men in grey

were blown apart in different ways. Death
flew about, like startled birds, alighting on one
man after another with shot and sabre,
bayonet and bullet. See here, two soldiers
run each other through at the same time,
each with a look of agonised astonishment

at what they've done and had done to them.
It was even-stevens a lot of the time
in the American Civil War. And anti-war
protesters were on the streets in US
and UK cities. The American Embassy,
in Grosvenor Square, was besieged with

protesters who were charged by mounted
police. It was all a bit like the American
Civil War. In the playground we swopped
rare cards and with the spares played
flick cards against a wall, gathering up
winnings like fallen leaves, while a chill

wind blew around our knees. There was
a lot of mud and rain in the American
Civil War cards; people got soaked through,
I felt right at home. In one scene a little boy
is hanged as a spy; he looked a bit like me,
it made me feel sad, I guess that's what

it was meant to do. The Civil War cards
were very energetic; the fighting was always
close, shooting at one another at point-blank
range, or stabbing each other with sword
and bayonet or anything sharp that came
to hand. That wasn't like the Vietnam War

where most of the time Marines seemed to fire
at a phalanx of grass and ranks of trees. The dry
rattle of their weapons was like a woodpecker
hammering bark. In one card Stonewall Jackson,
prominent on a white horse, is shot dead by his
own men. I knew, then, it would all be downhill.

It happened a lot, in Vietnam, that they shot
their own. In my mind the two wars happened
at the same time. In one card two wounded
soldiers help one another out; one wears blue,

the other grey, but it doesn't matter at the end
of the day. One tips water from his canteen into

the mouth of the other; now the fighting's over.
And then they showed this photo of a Marine
giving a Vietcong a drink from his canteen. Later
I heard it was faked, the Marine didn't want to do it;
he was ordered to pose to make a good photo –
which it did, for a while. At the end General Lee

sits at a shiny table and signs the surrender. He looks
sad, and I felt sad too. His white hair and beard
framed his stoic leathery face; he looked tired, which is
not surprising. It was quite an education, the American
Civil War in Bubblegum Cards. Like the bubblegum
it left a funny taste, unpleasant and enduring.

Movie Theatres

The movie theatres of childhood are uninhabited,
    like an old suit they no longer fit.
Only ghosts fill the foyers and never buy a ticket;
    and the seats creak in discomfort.
The flickering light no longer carries images; just
    picks out motes in a moulting world
as the wraiths discuss the storyline again in a
    loud voice. The ceiling leaks and the exit
signs no longer illumine a pathway to elsewhere.
    The double-bill leaves us unfulfilled;
the intermission is ripe with disappointment. The girl
    with a tray slung around her neck
has nothing to sell but a smile that vanishes as soon
    as you look at it. All her Choc Ices
have melted, her Poppets carry a white bloom, and her
    Kia-Ora's run dry. The Malteser boxes
have lost their rattle and the cigarettes carry no warnings.

Nameplate

Clunk! went the machine. A satisfying masculine sound.
Old and battered, even when I was a kid, it stood
Loitering patiently on the station platform like an
Inveterate trainspotter. A coin-operated, dial-driven,
Nameplate stamping machine. For a small fee it would

Produce, in painfully thin embossed strips of grey metal,
Indelible evidence of your own identity. Unfortunately, we
Never found a use for these gun-metal dog-taggy tokens,
Knowing little of our destiny but the names bequeathed us.

Hammersmith Flyover

You spread your wings above me and obscure the sky.
Newly built, your concrete arms reached up to heaven,
solemn and ecstatic hierophants to modern transportation.

Was it atavism, some pagan memory, that led to rumours
when I was a kid, that during construction East End gangsters
disposed of rivals' bodies inside your freshly poured concrete?

It's one way of being useful and probably not true but every time
I go past I see your cubic feet as so many upright coffins holding
a hidden human void beneath the perpetual thunder of traffic.

The Lions in Trafalgar Square

The lions in Trafalgar Square are weary
of being climbed on by too many tourists.
Always patient, they wait, with neat paws
stretched before them, for the rain to stop.
They've stayed too long beyond the end
of the party. The Empire they were made
to celebrate has packed up and gone.
But still the lions pose for photographs
at the four corners of a world no longer
pink, offer an elegant profile that clings
to dignity despite the occasional pigeon
poised on the head like a satirical comment.
Perhaps they dream of taking a trip, getting
out of town, leaving not even a shadow
behind, as they embark on a little holiday,
hitting the news as they roam the countryside,
maybe go and visit Frome in Somerset, where
long ago they were born into an optimistic
age of industry, in a foundry now closed.
Anyone can dream, even a bronze lion.
Back in Trafalgar Square the lions continue
to purr with a broad West Country burr.

St Paul's

Christopher Wren's imported Italian pulchritude
was somehow magicked into a northern latitude.

How high you float above the London sky
hemmed now by steel and glass high-rise.

Your dome a maternal breast to bless the city,
there to suckle both the needy and greedy.

Surrounded now by traffic and protestors,
you witness solemn rites and sharp investors.

Smoke clad in wartime, isolated and enflamed,
symbol of London, you survived unscathed.

Now a sentinel wrapped in the morning mist
as I struggle to work among all the rest.

When I enter your space I feel like an intruder
dwelling in the breast of holiness like a tumour.

Ode to Another Crisis

By the waters of Leman I sat down and wept …

T. S. Eliot, *The Waste Land,* line 182

The fiscal shuttle clacks day and night. The banking system
weaves its threads, on invisible looms, across the oceans,
around the earth, nations stretch on the warp and weft
of global debt. And now it seems we cannot conceive
any pattern apart from this fabric that binds us tight.
The stranglehold of avarice, elegant in kid-gloves,
will casually squeeze its fingers around our throat.
Advertising, so enticing, convinces us we need many
fleeting things. Mere dreams to feed a profit margin,
with goods made elsewhere, out of sight, in conditions
we'd rather not know about. The financiers bang the drum.
Everyone feels the lash and obeys the signal to row harder.
Governments pretend to steer the ship while bankers advise
them how to avoid reefs of their own invention; provide
proof the onus is on pay 'restraint'; make thousands
homeless and throw themselves another juicy bonus.

The Raft of the Medusa

hangs in the Louvre, its cargo of corpses, glinting
beneath brown varnish, like celebrities caught
in a reality TV programme, permanently on pause.

The canvas is indeed so big, in an emergency we could
actually use it as a raft, float down the Seine, astonish
the flâneurs as we wave from our improvised bateau.

Let's run through the salons, like cool sixties movie
icons, not care how many tourists we knock over,
in our race to prove we are still able to misbehave.

Still Life with Goat's Skull

Goat's Skull, Bottle and Candle by Pablo Picasso, 1952

Now the colour has gone out of everything,
skull, bottle and candle emerge from the twilight
glints of a grisaille world where white burns
with an artificial incandescence like the glow
of Roman candles. Imperious,

the bottle is quiet, mysterious,
its shadows concealing as much
as revealing – its candle a flower blooming light
that bursts like a flash bulb of astonishment
that this is all that's left.

There is agitation in the still life
and still life in the agitation – the goat's
horns writhe as though animated by
Grünewald's hell-bristled brush.

The empty eye socket glares at us –
'Who you looking at?' it snaps;
as the skull bone flares its angry nostrils
and haphazard teeth snap shut
on our minds.

Rembrandt: *Self Portrait*

Glints of the self emerge, here and there,
stand out from the midst of all that's hidden.
The struggle between darkness and light,
every revealing itself a new concealing.

His deft wrist applies the paint, thicker here,
thinner there, so many hues, more than the eye
can hold. Is this his art? To depict the invisible,
hold up a mirror where each viewer becomes

the subject, whatever it may be, can feel the wet
lick of brush summon the tingle of skin. There is
more to seeing than looking and no end to seeking.

Those quizzical brows, those desolate eyes, pose
questions with no answers. A masque of riddles.
A game of charades. Another dance in the dark.

Charred Beloved

i.m. Arshile Gorky

A nose, an eye, a lip,
all that is left of my beloved.
A smell, a smile, a laugh,
all that I hold of my beloved.
A cry, a tale, a lap,
all that I know of my beloved.

The dark, the light, the lonely
soul that longs
for a kiss from those
red red lips;
all that there is
to warm me.

Forgetting the past,
turning my back,
learning to love
a long new day
is all the hope
my brush can hold.

Blow the smoke from
my eyes, lift the lids
on tomorrow,
remake and renew
a past forged
from sorrow.

Farewell my beloved,
all your limbs are ash;
farewell my beloved,
all your passion cold;
farewell my beloved,
all your colour gone.

And now the milkweed weaves
a gentle wreath around my neck.

Five Painters

Giotto

A perfect O free hand
feet flat on the land
beneath a solid blue sky.

Piero

Eyes that stare through
resurrect sacred geometry's
plumb line to the unseen.

Leonardo

Within a deluge of lines
forms of life coalesce
but will never be finished.

Rembrandt

The weight of a life
held within the viscous
glisten of a brush stroke.

Pollock

The way life brimmed up
it was bound to get spilt
but left skeins of beauty.

Frank O'Hara in the Kitchen at 791 Broadway, 1963

Frank's in the kitchen, on the phone,
with a drink and a cigarette,
stacked dishes, pots and lids,
he leans against the door jamb – listening.
He and the phone cord describe a sixty-degree
angle, the better to see the world aslant.
The long cord loops and loops
around and around – a dancer
made of elastic words pulled
out of the air like a conjuror's paper flowers.
Frank and the telephone are one;
he is the receiver, picking up messages,
deciphering the mating call of car horns,
the Braille confidences of the subway grates,
and beneath his hands he marries everything.
The concupiscence of the world flows
like electric current through his fingers
and lands on the keys of his typewriter
with that sexy clatter, clat, clat.

Canary on the Balcony

For Enfield

There's a canary
on the balcony spilling songs
from his beak – like light from a tiny yellow sun.

And the bars of his cage are no barrier to his music
which swoops across the air – like aerial acrobats. He finds
so much to praise so much to grace with his song.

Inside his arias I too can fly – released at last
like a celebration of birds
from gravity's cage.

A Peal of Bells

The bells rest, silent, immovable, among the rafters;
they sleep in towered seclusion.
It is unthinkable that they should speak, as if a rock
were to ask the time or a tree
match one's stride through shadows of the forest.
But as I watch I imagine them stirring, swaying
as in a breeze, and see them heft
themselves up and roll back their tongues to lick a note,
hammer sound into a bright ball,
toss it out to awaken those who slumber too long below.
A solitary clang speaks of the forlorn but together
they join in joyous conversation,
and tumble about each other, acrobats of sound,
so happy to be together.

Two Memories of St Ives

In St Ives I queued for Roskilly's ice cream,
orange and mascarpone in a waffle cone,
pale as fresh snow, flecked with piquant
pieces of orange zest. Soft and creamy
beneath my tongue, a gentle tangy after-
taste. I licked it as I strolled along the quay.

As I raised it to my lips a seagull swooped
and swallowed the ice cream whole
leaving me holding nothing but cone.
It flew off with my orange and mascarpone
in its gullet. I must admit I wish it ill.
I hope it gets an ice cream headache.

In St Ives I visited Hepworth's house.
In the garden her sculpture blooms among
bamboo, a bronze budding grove, a glow
in the crystal coastal light that invites
long gazes. A garden of rooms, secret
glimpses, opening doors in imagination.

And here's a photograph of Hepworth
resting in the shade, leaning against
a plinth, light speckled, cigarette poised
between victorious fingers, far-off look.
Always smoking, thinking, smoking,
making. The solitude of a last cigarette

searching for connexions. She died
in a fire, like Ingeborg Bachmann,
another lost heroine, smoking in bed,
a dangerous companion. Spontaneous
combustion – a final smoke ring
unfurls in my mind – spelling O

Fruits of the Sea

Breakfast on the beach at Greatstone –
    a flask of tea and a fruit scone.
It's December and the sea is a grey seal
    relaxing on its back in the swell.
The wind is still, air languid, as the hoar
    waves gently lick the shore.
The strand is littered with coastal refuse –
    high tide's coughed up mucus.

Water-logged wood, plastic sheeting, flayed
    rope and abandoned shells.
Sitting by the dunes, whose wooden paling,
    easeful, cradles my back,
I gaze into the distance, where Dungeness
    Lighthouse winks at me
sharing secrets of the power station that
    I promise not to reveal.

Birling Gap

On the lolling hills above Birling Gap
the hawthorns bend into Art Deco
shapes beneath the prevailing wind.
Chalk cliffs march into the zenith;
serrated edges gnawing at the sky.
Sunlight, reflected off the chalk,
dazzles like a geological searchlight.

The cool grin of the cliffs displays layers
of flint embedded within the chalk,
amalgam fillings in otherwise perfect teeth.
Face to face with these strata of rock,
confronted by calcified time, I recall
the seasons shared on this beach,
and all the weathers it wore before me.

Every layer contains a living history
of past times, coals gone cold now on
beach fires that once danced in flame.
Taut expectations, whose glowing embers
conjure images that flicker like grainy film
into the present, here, on the beach, where
the cliffs cradle time in a pale embrace.

Bexhill Breakwater

The breakwater is shoed and girt in iron,
the wood planed bone smooth by the sea.
The iron blossoms a deep orange-russet
blistered by the slick lips of the waves.

Down the shore the groynes raise
their knobbly fingers, hushing the sea,
but the waves come and go regardless
about their rhythmic lunar business

to thunder among the shingle and
froth at the mouth as they swallow
the breakwaters; taking their time
to savour each arboraceous mouthful.

Bunker Archaeology

Along the coast the blockhouses maintain
their vigilance. Blank concrete faces stare
at the sea, half-buried in sands of memory.

A cold channel wind blows through gun slits.
As I peer out the breeze punches me in the eye.
Take that! it says, flâneur and trespasser beware.

Above there's a barrage of sea birds squawking
warnings to keep off. I need solace but the arms
of the wind are too cold and clasp without care.

From a distance the smooth bunkers look like
eggshells but are thicker, far thicker, containers
not of new life but tombs to outdated obsessions.

Close to they have their own hidden landscape,
pitted like smallpox survivors, abrading finger-
tips, turning a cheek, repulsing touch with grit.

Rusty streaks blemish the concrete, spreading
varicose veins of oxidation. Weeds grow freely,
spread satirical comments on ideas of permanence.

The wind kisses everything regardless of origin
or purpose. Always an invisible presence, arch
collaborator, and cruel shapeshifter of memory.

Caleb Nye

keeper of the town clock, Bexhill-on-Sea,
died punctually at eleven o'clock on the
eleventh day of the eleventh month.

Days wind down as surely as the spring
of the clock he wound up. He looks
out, defiant, at the viewer, peering

from bushy white brows, seafaring
beard, hands on hips, as if to bar entry.
There is certainty in his four-square stance.

He knows where he stands as surely
as he knows the time. But what if that
door behind him opened for a moment

and let something unexpected in?
But for now there are no surprises;
he holds the key that regulates time,

believes he has tamed it, can always
keep it harnessed in steady pace,
even sometimes make it chime.

Poetry Library

Elegy for Ted Hughes

Your words are hewn like stone,
arranged
      one on
          another,
like drystone walls, they balance
with only each other to hold them up;
but look as if they've been there
            for all eternity.

I imagine your hands must often
have been sore from lifting so many
heavy, jagged, flint-edged words.

There was always a chill wind
blowing through your verse;

as I speak it
      I can feel it
          chap my lips.

All those animals you wrote about:
the Hawk, the Pike, the Jaguar,
the Crow, were they all
      just totems of you?

When you knew you were dying
you finally published what we had all
been waiting for; and what did
      it say?

She was too quick on the draw
      for you
and went clean through you,
      like a silver bullet,
to vanquish your werewolf spirit;
      but it happened so fast
you didn't know you were dead
      for a long time.

The Taste of Home

For Amjad

It is rainy. It is spring, and my friend remembers
the olive harvest in his village in Palestine before
everything changed. The streets deserted, everyone who is able out in the groves picking olives.

But at night the village throngs with life. In the cool
of the evening they queue at the communal press.
He remembers the taste of freshly squeezed olive oil
on freshly baked bread. It is a long way from there

to this noisome London street or even to a quiet
city park where we sit and talk about poetry.
Some day he will return. His memory is the key
to unlock the doors of yesterday and tomorrow.

The Old Ballroom, Berlin

We have all seen better days, my dear.
The ballroom ceiling is falling in,
The crystal chandelier, Damoclesian,
Hangs by a thread above our heads.
Under our feet pellets of fallen plaster
Crunch beneath our boots, sounding
Like hardened bubbles of hope bursting.
We have all seen better days, my dear.
So many heel leads that never led to love.
So many New Year's Eves whose promise
Evaporated along with the morning dew.
But the duende of dance still presides
Over this room of rhythmic pleasure,
Whose many supplicants, multiplied,
Haunt its foxed and dappled mirrors.
We have all seen better days, my dear.

Hearthless

The mating dragonflies are unaware of brevity
copulating in mid-air in defiance of gravity.
The present is a glint on a bird's beak, the frenzied
beat of wings. Time is a trapeze on which we swing
between past and future, defying the weight
of the past, as the upswing propels us into
a future full of all the past there's going to be.

Ownerless time unfolds without us, emptying hour-glass
after hour-glass, like a man with a thirst he cannot quench.
And we alight on place after place, pausing only long
enough to know we have been there before and have
to move on, seeking that flash of light, which opens
the world like a blade, but is always just out of sight.

Warming hands before imaginary embers we conjure
words. Naming things preserves them but changes
their flavour and the unnamed slips from our grasp.
The mating dragonflies are unaware they know all
they know; but what they know they know so well.

The Double

He follows me around,
hasn't got a life of his own,
but uses bits of mine instead.

He picks out moments,
rummaging through the
dustbin of memories.

He's expert at identity theft,
living on credit cards he knows
he'll never have to pay.

He's stolen my fingerprints
and now everything he
touches incriminates me.

He has no backbone but uses mine
to crawl around the house; he
is still an invertebrate at heart.

I'll get him in the end, catch him
in the act of impersonation, confront
him and say: Who do you think you are?

And he'll say: I thought you were me –
so what does that make you?

Elegy for NYC

Six weeks after 9/11 I flew into the gap-toothed city. When the
wind blew from downtown you could catch the sweet smell of
barbecued meat, still on the broil. At Ground Zero the sallow JCBs
reached in with their long limbs to claw at the tangled wreckage;
and flames leapt into the air, freed from their underground oven.

All around every building was deserted; a thick layer of dust
covered every surface. Between the devastation and the harbour
lay a refugee city of makeshift shrines to the lost; people who
went to work, just like any other day. Now they smile from photos
taken in an entirely different world. Words of grief settle on them,

like dust, evoke emotions landing deep in the solar plexus.
Around the corner, in the multi-storey parking lot, the patient cars
await their owners' return. They all look alike under their shroud
of dust; no matter how long they wait, no one comes to claim them.

What's the Time?

What's the time Mr Wolf?

It's the time when cherry blossom
dances on the breeze.
It's the time when buds poke out
noses and sniff the air.
It's the time when politicians make promises
some even they think they'll keep.
It's the time when the slits in ballot boxes
accept our slender offerings.

What's the time Mr Wolf?

It's the time when distant thunder
sounds like guns.
It's the time when guns like lightning
illuminate the sky.
It's the time to be going on foot or in trucks
taking what you can carry.
It's the time for memories to lie buried
in the rubble of homes.

What's the time Mr Wolf?

It's the time to harvest the crops
but no one dares.
It's the time to blow the chaff from
mortar bombs and IEDs.
It's the time to run and smash all the
grandfather clocks.
It's the time to unfasten the watches
from dead men's wrists.

What's the time Mr Wolf?

It's the time to stop asking
stupid questions.
It's dinner time and I'm going
to eat you up.

Adlestrop or Elsewhere (1914 or 2014)

i.m. Edward Thomas

It's four a.m. and the blackbirds' arias begin
Summoned from restless sleep the air rings
Like a bell as the trees blossom with song
And natural music cleaves the air like a fin
      in Adlestrop or elsewhere
But there's another reveille over the horizon
As Russian tanks hiss and clank into Ukraine
And the AK47s unzip the air around Baghdad
Still the blackbirds invent theme and variation
      in Adlestrop or elsewhere
Everyone squabbles over territory even the birds
Salutations incriminations mating and nesting
There is no rest even at four a.m. the dawn listens
Holds its breath as distant songs are barely heard
      in Adlestrop or elsewhere
And the search for peace is strangely wrought
There's a web in which everyone seems fixed
All hasten to do what they think they should
But the cost is far more than anyone thought

Some Assembly Required

He comes back to her
     from Afghanistan

She assembles the bits
     artificial left leg
artificial right arm
     artificial right leg

Now he is complete again
     sometimes he reminds her
of the meccano set her father
     treasured as a child

But nonetheless he is
     all hers

He is the best easy-assemble
     husband she could
have imagined
     and all the parts work

Return of the Warrior

Like some inverted Odysseus
he comes back from the war
and does not recognise himself.

His body is whole but he left
so many parts of his mind in Helmand
he fears he'll never find them again.

He can no longer bear
the company of those
who were closest to him.

There's a minefield now between
his touch and theirs that he can't
quite figure out how to cross.

His reflection is lost
behind the plate glass
of high street shops.

The ghost of retail therapy
has run out of credit but still
hangs around the displays.

His hand instinctively clenches
on nothing again and again
crushing it into a solid ball of anger.

He staggers inside
the crowd's clangour
like a man in a storm.

In the mall he attracts attention, smirks
and laughs, from youths who watch
him flinch from blows no one can see.

Darkness Spoken

Darkness speaks.
His teeth glint, his spittle flies.
Darkness speaks with confidence.
He turns out the light the better for us to see him.
Darkness speaks with passion.
Like a conjurer producing a bouquet of paper flowers
he unveils resentment in every breast.
Darkness speaks with renewed vehemence.
He knows where you live and who you love.
He counts every moment you don't conform.
He cultivates your cowardice.
Darkness speaks.
No one argues.
No one dares.

Arrears

i.m. Ingeborg Bachmann

War is no longer declared
but takes place everywhere.
In streets and cafés, in offices and shops, war speaks.
Everyone is in uniform
whether they know it or not.
Marching is compulsory, but no one minds,
they think this is their natural gait.
Hearts are mortgaged to the hilt.
We've run out of credit.
Soon the bailiffs will call
and remove that worthless pound of palpitating flesh.

Resistance Poet

i.m. Jean Cassou

The words come to him in the dark, flit like bats
about his head. They are strangely comforting.
In solitary, he unwraps them like a gift, arranges
them, in a line, in his mind. And so, time passes.
He juggles words in his head, inscribing them
in his memory, like scratched messages on a
cell wall. And so, time passes, momentarily
free from anxiety, free from the criss-cross net
of prison galleries; free from the jingle-jangle
of gaoler's keys; free from the resonant slap
and scratch, slap and scratch, of boot on stone.
The word game becomes a gift to give to others;
it becomes a hope for a future. His imagination
carries him beyond the shackles of his cell, beyond
the yard, the walls, the gates, and up, up, up, into
the air, where he can see so much further than before.

The Well

The well head draws me near, a magnet to my curiosity,
its white clerical collar a full stop that halts my walk.
The well has a deep root that takes me down to depths
I sense but cannot see. Whatever's there dowses me.

The well observes the sky with an unblinking eye. The rain
raises a Braille message on its iris I am too blind to read.
It watches the slow clouds torn apart and when I peer down
I tip, sucked weightless by its grip, until I come to again.

I could squander my time mesmerised by this mirror but I
turn away, unplug my gaze from its face, take as my cue
its upward stare, rise up and taste the wind. And stand,
a pair of solitary bellows, stranded between earth and sky.

Circus of Cruelty

La Poupée (1936) by Hans Bellmer

Dis-articulate doll deprived of choice
designed depraved without a voice.

Posed provocation twisted left for dead
displayed delectation sad broken head.

Unable to turn away a fixated stare
echoes obsession says viewer beware.

Invited to witness this our own crime scene
masks ripped off prove us worse than we seem.

If you could speak what would you tell?
A fairy-tale that casts a molten spell.

A thousand nights of fever brought you forth
from fervent glimpses to miraculous birth.

Your lips are sealed but you speak so clear
those who can listen are drawn ever near.

Lee Miller in Hitler's Tub

Lee Miller takes a wash in Hitler's tub:
her boots stand sentry before it, leather
and buckles sag, weary from clambering
over the smoking wreckage of Europe.

Miller looks up and back as if to glimpse
who is coming in the door, friend or foe?
Her hand, immersed in a flannel, rubs the
dust from ruined cities off her shoulder.

Her wristwatch lies, prudently abandoned,
on a stool; the time is nineteen-forty-five.
A photograph of Hitler, stiff and formal,
out of focus, as befits the newly dead,

sits propped on the edge of the tub, as if
observing this surprising visitor from afar.
It will remain a mystery why Hitler
needed no less than three soap dishes.

The Cobblestones of Berlin

The cobblestones of Berlin form a constellation
beneath my feet; every one is unique, and so small
they can fit into the palm of my hand, but together
they carry the weight of the city. Each unregarded
stone remains, day after day, always the same.
The marching feet are no longer in the street,
but something hammers on the door of my mind.
The stones are silent, though I know there's much
they could say. The sun, the rain and the sleet,
laughter and tears, all wash over them. Outside
my apartment at Heinrich-Roller-Strasse 7,
a stumbling-block stands out, its gold tooth glint
arrests among the rest; a reminder of former times
when history stopped and rapped on the door.

HERE LIVED
ILSE DOROTHEA
SCHMIDT
NEE JACOBY
BORN 1902
ARRESTED 24.12.1942
DEPORTED 1943
MURDERED IN
AUSCHWITZ

Forest Swastika

The beauty of design deceives;
larches planted in a pine forest
go unnoticed most of the year
but every autumn change colour
and become the broken arms
of a golden swastika. Ablaze
atop the canopy, a living emblem
flails the sky, declaiming again
a stealthy "Sieg Heil! Sieg Heil!"

> When they pull
> the starter cord
> Ka-zetnik! Ka-zetnik!
> The chainsaws
> clear their throats
> Ka-zetnik! Ka-zetnik!
> spit petrol fumes,
> blow blue smoke.

Inside, the dark wood keeps its
secrets, holds its hidden patterns
that survive unnoticed year on year
while rodents scamper and rummage
dead leaves, disturbing the shades
that dwell within this pungent
spoor of memory. No Reich lasts;
now the trees are culled and they
must pay the price of their nativity.

> When they pull
> the starter cord
> Ka-zetnik! Ka-zetnik!
> The chainsaws
> clear their throats
> Ka-zetnik! Ka-zetnik!
> spit petrol fumes,
> blow blue smoke.

Now there is a new "selection";
the larches are the chosen.
The chainsaws' screams
ignite the birds into flight
to circle in the dying light.
One by one the larches fall;
sawdust spills from their trunks,
like the blood of the innocents,
and smoke drifts upward again.

The Forest Swastika was located near Zernikow in northeastern Germany. KZ was the Nazi abbreviation for Konzentrationslager (Concentration Camp) and inmates were often referred to as Kazetniks.

The Water Clock

That leaking tap is a water clock keeping me
awake – busy account counting moments.
Morsels of memory float to the surface
like soggy crusts in the washing-up.
I stir my hand in the greasy water
to see if anything else comes up.
I am waiting for a revelation
that always arrives too late.
A moment when all will
be open, all will be
known, alighting
on the palm of
the mind.

Dawn Prayer

In the two-up, two-down of conscience
        there lurks a nasty smell.
Something's gone bad in the larder,
        something climbs up the well.
There stands superego, that stern
        slave master with a whip.
The night visions offer just a glimpse,
        hints that vanish too quick.
There's something climbing up the stairs,
        tapping gently on the walls;
I'd get up and open wide the door but
        I'm paralysed and appalled
at what my mind will next invent to bring
        me to my knees, a penitent
with no prayer to my lips, no promised
        salvation immanent.
But the dawn comes after all, late and
        flushed, the morning light
seeps through the pane and frees
        the prisoner of the night.

God's Nightmare

Sometimes I am so glad to wake and be free at last
of those cruel, illogical but relentless dreams.

What if the world is a nightmare dreamt by God?
What if he can't wake up and the dream goes on and on?

What if his imagination is vast as the ocean and the dream
boundless, self-renewing, from which there is no release?

What would it look like, this eternal dream?
Careful, look around, would it not look like this?

Imaginary Cartography

I'm drawing myself a map in order to get out of here,
I'm heading towards the border in order to cross over.

I don't need a passport in the land I've made;
no visas hem me in; no quotas keep me out.

And besides I've got the map, it shows me where to go,
how to evade people and places I don't want to know.

Folded into its contours are the gradients of love;
cairns of loss; the icy breath of the hidden crevasse.

I'm founding a new alphabet, unearthing new meanings,
tucked under strange tongues I'm learning to decipher.

There are games of hide-and-seek in the mountains
and forests, places to get lost in, places to be found.

And in one corner I've put *Here be dragons*. I'm drawing myself
a map – I'm getting out of here – sooner than anyone thinks.

Quick Quick Slow

i.m. Mark Strand

Listen.   There it is again.
The sound of the world grinding gears
changing down as if about to tackle
a long steep hill.

Listen.   Everything's slowing.
The birds have forgotten their tunes
no one can remember their purpose
even if they had one.

Listen.   The light is going.
The mirror is always empty now
no one steps in no one steps out
mist fills the pane.

Listen.   There is still time.
Pretend it's all right let's squeeze in
one last dance put your hand on my
shoulder follow my lead.

Eating Cloudberries on Torghatten

Torghatten rises from the North Sea,
a Napoleonic hat, atop the head
of a stone giant immersed beneath
the Nordic waves. It's the mountain
with the hole in the middle, so big,
one time a daredevil flew a plane through it.
The hole was eroded by the motion of water
long before we existed to behold it.
Now we strain our necks to gaze up
at the cathedral immensity of its space.
Massive, rugged, sun swept, Torghatten
looms over the archipelago like a whale
surrounded by little fish. And we are
just barnacles on its crust as we ascend
towards the sun. In July heat we clamber up,
over the granite rocks and skin-thin layer of soil.
We are caressed by the light and air,
and the breeze gives us a sweet kiss.
As we climb we pick wild cloudberries
and eat them. The sun baked them on the bush;
the amber berries are hot in the mouth and taste
the way the cuisine in nature's own kitchen should.
At the top, light-headed, the vista spreads
below us, a scattered jigsaw of land and sea;
the taste of wild cloudberries still on the tongue.

Sleeping Beauty, Norway

Along a mountain path
        something bright
        attracts my eye
glimpsed through the arms
of twisted boughs and leaves
        she sits alone
        a forgotten deity.
Abandoned at the bottom
        of a ravine this
curvaceous fifties pick-up truck
        reclaimed by nature
        turned orange russet
        with the tint of rust
        glows with mystery
like an exotic metal flower.
Solitary in her abandonment
she dreams of empty highways
        endless blacktops
        smooth as skin
        while she waits
like a sleeping beauty
        for her prince
        to awaken her.

Three Girls on a Bridge

Girls on the Bridge by Edvard Munch, 1899

Three girls stand on the bridge,
each gazes down at the water;
what is it they see float before
them that silences all chatter?

In the watery ink, that Keats knew
too soon will surely disappear
like the fleet song of birds, do they
see a faint future written there?

Perhaps they are trying on possible
lives, like suits of clothes, eager
for a mirror as they try to glimpse
how they look in one or another?

All is yet to be. The sky amorphous,
the river reflecting what they mostly
know already. A familiar world made
invisible when clutched too closely.

Their taut postures and hunched
shoulders suggest a restless quest
for more than a small town can
offer, some yet unseen happiness.

St Kateri Tekakwitha

Kateri Tekakwitha
Iroquois saint
you stand outside
St Patrick's Cathedral
New York City
your eyes shut
head tilted up
as if listening
for a divine
radio transmission
you ignore the traffic
offer your open palms
to each passer-by
tempt them to touch
the cup of openness
your fingers make.
Lily of the Mohawks
you knew how to
bridge the space
between
each and each
now and eternity
earth and sky
weave us into your light
like a thread of hair
in one of your braids
so that we might rest
gently on your breast
one of many strands
stronger
more beautiful
together.

Stylite

pinnacle of aspiration
rusty nail of faith
hammered into the desert
neck stretched to heaven
flesh left to wind and sun
sinews strung like a bow
feet fastened on your perch
high above us
you never look down
your ascent is our prayer
unswerving ambition
sun-flayed
rain-sharpened
raw-sensed
and ready to loose
the arrowhead
of your devotion
to pierce suffering
here on this plain where
you show up for miles
a solitary I
on the blank page
of the sky
a living monument
surfing the tide of spirit
our nourishment
our holy radio mast
always tuned in.

St Veronica

Dear Veronica, you of the Instamatic Veil,
I loved the paintings of you
in museum, gallery or church.
There I'd find your gentle face a peaceful interlude
among all that martyrdom.
The painter's images are made
only with paint whereas yours
was made with perspiration
and magic. There you stand
holding up your veil
lightly at the edges,
like a freshly developed photograph
whose alchemy is still wet,
so that we can see His face.
He is a fish caught in the net of existence
just passing through but
He left this trace behind
much like modern tourists
who feel compelled to take
a snapshot of themselves
at every place they visit
against the day when they
can no longer believe
they'd once been there at all.

Salmon's Leap

Something in the salmon makes her leap the falls
time and again, against the flow, she ascends
one cascade at a time. Between the falls she rests,
just below the surface, slow and luminous, scales
shimmering in the light, gills pumping like a panting
mouth and I hold my breath as I watch, but then
my shadow falls across her and she is gone, fleeting
as words that flash across my mind but cannot settle.

Lanyon Quoit, Cornwall

The naked barrow cradles air; whatever precious
cargo lay there has long since disappeared.

The bones that remain are stones that shape
a chamber to the dead. Now the only necromancy

is a tourist homage to the past. A long lost form
of life lies buried beyond the horizon of imagining.

All is light and air across the moor. The wind
kisses everything without exception. The stones,

lichen wrapped, make offerings to the sky, without
ceasing, unblinking, awaiting the ancestors return.

Dragonflies

Dragonflies hover in imagination
long after they disappear – dart past
on fragile wings – stitch time
into an eternal instant.

The lake is a restless mosaic
of dots and dashes –
a Morse Code message
spelled in light.

Here all is made bright –
glints on the needlepoint of time –
to vanish once more
in an eye blink.

For Magritte, on a Rainy Day

Thanks to Jaroslav Seifert for the umbrella

This is not an umbrella.

But when is a poem
not an umbrella?
Why, when it's raining
of course!

At other times a poem
is always an umbrella,
ready to give shelter
within its papery embrace.

And though its body may be thin,
at our touch it will begin
to unfurl new worlds
of possibility.

Provided, of course,
it is not raining.